FAITH IN ALCOHOLICS ANONYMOUS

By A Bill Friend

FAITH IN ALCOHOLICS ANONYMOUS

A Bill Friend

Cover designed by Thomas J Laperriere

A Bill Friend
Visit my website at www.abillfriend.com

Printed in the United States of America

First Printing: March 2019
History of Recovery

ISBN-13 978-1-6455010-8-4

Table of Contents

Part One: Visceral Belief and Faiths Plural

101 Wanting to Stop; Finding You Cannot

What sick alcoholic doesn't want to stop drinking? Most alcoholics have tried to stop many times. They have tried many ways to free themselves from alcoholism. They want freedom from alcohol, but powerful forces deep within their personalities keep them trapped. They want to stop, but find they cannot.

Strange as this may sound, these people who want to stop *believe* they *must* drink alcohol. If they believed something else, they would do something else.

Ask why someone did something and the reply is likely to be, "At the time I believed it was the thing to do." Every time alcoholics drink, it is because they believe it is the thing to do at that time. Understanding this behavior motivating type of belief gives us insight into just about everything people do. Belief is how our personalities operate.

Faith is an important feature of human personality. To truly understand faith requires an explanation of belief. Beliefs are the components that give rise to faith. We first gather the parts, then assemble the deeper concept. Let's look at belief and use what we find to understand faith.

102 Behavior Motivating Belief

Beliefs deep within us make us who we are and motivate what we do. Actively drinking alcoholics believe they must drink alcohol and sober alcoholics believe they must stay sober. These gut level visceral beliefs motivate our personalities and animate our behavior.

Behavior-motivating visceral beliefs are like breaths of air for the body. A single breath is vital in the moment we take it and gone the next. At all times we are doing what we believe we ought to be doing at that time. The belief of the moment motivates the behavior of the moment.

Visceral beliefs are the working of our instincts. Faith in a Higher Power is a lasting type of belief that develops from gut level instinctive belief. The beliefs that make up religious and other forms of faith are persistent beliefs.

Other examples of persistent beliefs are strong political views and the belief structure of active alcoholism. Alcoholics form persistent beliefs around alcohol and themselves that maintain the psychological side of alcoholism.

Visceral beliefs motivate individual actions. Persistent beliefs are responsible for habits and patterns of thought, feeling, and behavior. These two types of belief give rise to and reinforce each other. Individual behaviors become habits with repetition; patterns of activity keep us doing the things we do. Visceral and persistent beliefs together comprise the belief structure of our personalities.

We may desire to stop drinking and determine to try a method of treatment, but our attitude towards alcohol and ourselves sabotages our intention. Our experience of failure in all our past attempts at finding lasting freedom from alcohol creates a subconscious belief that for us sobriety is not possible. This persistent belief sabotages sincere attempts at recovery. It's one way the belief structure of active alcoholism keeps us trapped no matter how strong our desire to be free.

Often, alcoholics have had some awful experience that creates a strong desire to find lasting sobriety. They act on this desire and enter a treatment program. As they progress through the program, their deeper, more implicit beliefs operate beneath the surface. They begin to say what they believe will get them by in the program without realizing that this type of dishonesty is rooted in their subconscious belief that for them sobriety is not possible. They want to get well, but attitudes and habits established years ago when they were forced into treatment programs sabotage efforts now motivated by sincere desire. Very few alcoholics say they do not believe sobriety is possible for them, but this subconscious belief is a common component in the personality of many struggling alcoholics.

Beliefs that motivate our actions and lasting beliefs together occupy a controlling place in our personality. When we lose faith in the beliefs that motivate our alcoholism, it creates space in our personality for sober beliefs to motivate us. The sober beliefs displace alcoholic beliefs and become the controlling factor in our personality.

The desire to get over alcoholism must come from within. Alcoholism and sobriety operate at gut level, deep within our personalities. Examining the workings of belief within human personality is key to understanding alcoholism and empowering sobriety.

103 Faith Has an Object; Beliefs Have Content

The words faith and belief are close in casual meaning, and often used in ordinary conversation to say the same thing. There are important differences, however. Beliefs have content; we believe things. Faith forms around a collection of beliefs in a faith object. Faith in a Higher Power is one form of faith, faith in one's sponsor another. To have faith in something or someone does not necessarily mean to worship it. It means only that we have lasting confidence in it based on our beliefs.

As individual persons we like to believe that all our beliefs and everything we have faith in is true. This is often far from true of us. In reality, when falsehoods serve our purposes we tend believe them with greater vigor than truth.

Faith is not always a positive force in our personality; there are destructive forms of faith that operate in human personality. Alcoholic belief is one of them. The collection of beliefs alcoholics form around alcohol, drugs, themselves and their world is the destructive form of faith called alcoholic belief. This faith destructive maintains the roads to the alcoholics' destruction. Alcoholic faiths destructive beliefs sabotage the alcoholics various attempts at finding lasting sobriety and keep the alcoholic drunk.

Faith is a present lasting confidence in the object around which that faith has formed. It may become stronger or weaker, but it is always confidence. Faith in an object can collapse. But loss of faith is not always a bad thing. Alcoholics who lose faith in their excuses for drinking are likely to get well when presented with our solution to alcoholism.

Gut level activity motivating belief is momentary; after it has motivated, an activity belief in the next activity takes its motivating role. The words faith and belief describe different functions within human personality. Personality is intellect, emotion and will; with the will having two parts; desire and determination. Belief is personality in action. Our thinking, feeling, desiring, and determining reflect the confidences (faith) and motivations (beliefs) functioning in our personality.

People do not think and only think. All thought is also feeling, desiring, and determining. When the mind is most active, for clarity, we call this thinking and understand that the rest of our personality is involved. Or we can just call it belief. The same is true of emotion. Our minds and wills do not shut off. They are part of the emotion being experienced in our personality. We act emotionally when our beliefs motivate our feelings. The ever-changing motivations at work in our personality are beliefs.

Faith is the ever present and lasting part of our personality. We collect beliefs and they become faith in someone or something. A particular type of religious belief becomes faith in God. Faith is a collection of beliefs in a faith object.

For example, a recovering alcoholic believes complete abstinence is the only solution to alcoholism and fellowship is essential to recovery. Together, these and similar beliefs become faith in Alcoholics Anonymous. This faith is part of the alcoholics' spiritual recovery. It is one of several collections of beliefs that together motivate sobriety in the alcoholics' personality.

104 Faiths Plural

The Faiths Plural concept is part of a broad understanding of the role faith plays in recovery from alcoholism. Sober beliefs must displace the beliefs of active alcoholism for an alcoholic to get and stay sober.

In our culture, there is a tendency to think of only one form of faith at a time doing whatever happens to be the job at hand. In reality, it is belief in several forms of faith that gets and keeps alcoholics sober. Sobriety is maintained by nurturing these various forms of faith. Every sober alcoholic lives by several forms of faith.

When we list some of these forms of faith, we begin to see how the faiths plural concept works. Faith in ones Higher Power, confidence in one's decision to get well, and faith in Alcoholics Anonymous as well as other similar forms of faith together motivate sobriety.

Self-confidence, a form of faith in one's self, is a special part of the faiths plural concept. Alcoholism damages our self-esteem in ways that are similar to physical torture. People who mistreat others first break the self-confidence of those they are mistreating. Alcoholism does this, too. That ought to inform our understanding of cultivating a healthy self-confidence. Unhealthy selfishness should not be confused with healthy self-esteem and confidence in one's decision to participate in Alcoholics Anonymous.

The confusion and despair actively drinking alcoholics experience are the visible results of alcoholism's destruction of faith in one's self. A person without confidence in the decision to get well often falters. Many alcoholics struggle with an unconscious belief that sobriety is not possible for them. Encouraging alcoholics who seek our help to have faith that they can recover could save their lives.

Faith in one's Higher Power is the most important form of faith in the sober alcoholic's belief structure, but other forms of faith also play an essential role in recovery as well. A general faith in Alcoholics Anonymous is one form of sober belief. Alcoholics who believe in God as their Higher Power also have faith that the Alcoholics Anonymous program is the method for applying God's power.

Many newcomers have difficulty with the concept of God helping them. Alcoholics Anonymous, not the organization or the individuals, but the core idea of the program, which is recovery from alcoholism by complete abstinence, can stand in for God as a Higher Power. Faith in that idea can function as a Higher Power. The love of the fellowship for the suffering alcoholic is similar to the love of God.

Interpreting the core idea of the Alcoholics Anonymous program as an object of faith, one can insert the words Alcoholics Anonymous as a stand in for the word God in the 12 Steps. Anyone having difficulty with the word God can use the words Alcoholics Anonymous to stand in for God in the 12 Steps and get good results because of the similar role the Alcoholics Anonymous fellowship and program play in sobriety.

Both God and Alcoholics Anonymous set the ground rules for 12 Step recovery, complete abstinence from alcohol and substances that have similar effects. Both God and Alcoholics Anonymous care about the wellbeing of the alcoholic who still suffers. They work best together, but alcoholics for whom God is a problem can use only Alcoholics Anonymous as their Higher Power.

The fellowship's collective love for suffering alcoholics can stand in for the love of God. Like a Loving Higher Power, the fellowship wants suffering alcoholics to find sobriety and become again the people they are meant to be.

The role of God in the sobriety of an alcoholic taking the 12 Steps must be played by what stands in for God. In a theatrical production, an understudy steps in for an actor as necessary. Only an understudy who can play the role is capable of standing in. A Loving God wants the alcoholic to find life by abstaining from alcohol and substances that have similar effects. Alcoholics Anonymous may be an alternative borne of necessity, but it can play the role of Higher Power if necessary.

Many people who have problems with the "God part" of the 12 Steps believe that Alcoholics Anonymous can restore them to sanity. Members who use God as their Higher Power believe that, together with their faith in God. Often, those who have trouble with "the God stuff" at the beginning of the 12 Step process come out the other side as believers. Starting with a stand in Higher Power is a way to enable the process to begin with any alcoholic willing to work the 12 Steps.

Faiths Plural is an uncommon but accurate description of human behavior. It is how we all see the world. It is how alcoholics get and stay sober. The 12 Steps are crucial for recovery from alcoholism. Using Alcoholics Anonymous as one's Higher Power anyone can take the 12 Steps.

Part Two: Alcoholism as Faith Destructive

201 Exposure to Alcohol and the Allergy

Everything about alcoholism is rooted in the allergy. Alcoholics are born with brains hypersensitive to the pleasurable effects of alcohol on the human mind. This hyper sensitivity is the basis of the allergy.

The allergy is often misunderstood because most allergies cause a discomfort in the body. The mind, sensing the discomfort, reacts with repulsion. The discomfort creates a motivation to get away from the substance of the allergen.

The allergic reaction of alcoholism is the opposite. It's not uncommon for alcoholics to remember the first time they drank alcohol as a magical event. Non-alcoholics experience pleasure from drinking, but not of the type and intensity an alcoholic experiences. Non-alcoholics drink alcohol, sometimes just for pleasure, but confess they "don't like the way they feel if they have more than one or two drinks." We know not everyone who drinks alcohol becomes an alcoholic.

Upon first contact with alcohol, the brain of the alcoholic experiences extraordinary pleasure of great intensity. This pleasure overwhelms the alcoholic's entire personality. Exposure to alcohol activates alcoholism for those with a hypersensitive brain. Their personality changes, alcoholism has its foothold, and the changes are irreversible.

Those who find their entire personality overtaken by this first experience describe themselves as alcoholics from their first drink. Their behavior changes and they begin drinking as often as possible. In others, alcohol's foothold takes time to develop into what they describe as alcoholism.

Exposure during childhood to alcohol or similar substances can result in one becoming an alcoholic unawares. People so exposed have a strong desire to drink and get high from a very early age, and may even think they were born wanting to get drunk and get high.

Many alcoholics describe the pleasure of their first drink as a personality change. A person born with the hyper sensitivity who never used alcohol would not be considered an alcoholic. Alcoholics are born with the allergy, hypersensitivity to alcohol, and become alcoholics by drinking.

The alcoholic's brain experiences intense and extraordinary pleasure, which creates an intense physical craving for alcohol. These thoughts and motivations continue after the body is made sick by alcohol's effects. The hypersensitive brain exposed to alcohol is blind to the toxic nature of the drug; the brain cannot see as poison a thing it has an overwhelming desire for more of. A much greater sensitivity to the pleasurable effect of alcohol in the brains of alcoholics is the physical manifestation of the alcoholic allergy.

202 Powerless over Alcohol

In alcoholics, normal rational thought is disrupted by the effect of alcohol use on their brain. The brain is drugged by the alcohol. The intense pleasure blinds the mind to the body's sickness even as it creates strong demands for more of the drug. This allergic sensitivity and compulsion reaction is the source of every other bad effect of alcoholism.

Alcoholics in the grip of alcoholism may behave very badly, but are not responsible for being an alcoholic. The physical sensitivity of their brain to alcohol is the powerlessness of the alcoholic. Because its physical side is rooted in the brain, alcoholism is no more a choice than the color of one's eyes. Because alcoholics are physically powerless over alcohol, the only way to avoid being overpowered is to abstain from all use. All substitutes lead back to the real thing, so other addictive substances are to be avoided also.

Alcoholics are powerless because they are born with the brain chemistry that becomes alcoholism when exposed to alcohol and similar substances.

Many diseases begin before they are recognized. Actual alcoholism begins when the alcoholic's disease becomes activated by exposure. Alcoholics who do not have a perfect recollection of that experience may believe they spent the first years of their drinking controlling their alcoholism. A person with fully developed and obvious alcoholism is the mental picture most people, including alcoholics, have of alcoholism. Most alcoholics are skillful at hiding their alcoholism, and many never fit society's stereotypes.

Sober alcoholics should avoid abusing mood and mind altering drugs. Special care should be taken by alcoholics and their doctors when some medications are considered for use.

203 Compulsion Creates Mental Obsession

The mental result of most allergies is repulsion: clear it out and stay away from the allergen. The mental result of the alcoholism allergy is compulsion: the brain says give me more and when can I do this again.

The compulsion reaction is the source of the mental obsession. An obsession is an unusual mental trait that can develop in the human personality whereby a person becomes preoccupied with an idea, substance, or person.

The compulsive desire alcohol triggers in the alcoholic's brain creates an obsessive thought pattern, the determination to get more alcohol in every situation.

The mental obsession present in all alcoholics is an unusual personality trait that turns almost everything that happens to them into a reason to or an excuse for drinking. The alcoholic drinks when bored or excited. Excuses magically appear when the alcoholic needs a "reason" to drink. This is the mental obsession at work in the alcoholic's personality. With the mental obsession's help, alcoholics have an endless supply of reasons to drink alcohol and excuses for doing so.

204 Alcoholic Belief

One of the great mysteries of alcoholism is how its self-destructive behaviors become part of us, a sort of instinctive drive in our personality. The motivation to drink comes from within, like hunger or thirst. Alcoholism is similar to a natural human instinct.

The personality change when alcohol meets a hypersensitive brain is an imperative, belief-creating experience. All of our instincts are imperative beliefs, and parts of the core imperative belief, "I Must Thrive." We are all born with the will to live and an instinct to thrive.

A hidden part of the personality change created by exposure to alcohol is an addition to the alcoholic's instinctive drives. The onset of alcoholism creates an imperative belief that acts like an instinct. For alcoholics, drinking alcohol is second nature, and this is true in a literal sense.

For the normal person, thriving includes the imperative beliefs "I Must Eat," "I Must Find Shelter," "I Must Have Sex," and so on. The alcoholic has all of those, but "I Must Drink Alcohol" becomes part of thriving as well.

Securing food or sex and seeking shelter from the cold are physical responses driven by our instincts. Attached to many of our instincts is a physical cue that tells us to take the actions needed to thrive. Hunger is a cue. Sexual arousal is another. We respond to these cues by figuring out what we believe is the best way to satisfy our needs.

Humans are limited. In reality, our solutions are not always the best means to solve a problem. Our solutions are the ones we believe will solve the problem.

Every moment of our lives our instincts make demands on us. We respond to these demands by doing what we believe is best at that moment. We do not act in the way that is actually best; we act in the way that we believe is best. Understanding human belief is key to understanding human behavior. Our idea of best is not always good for us in the long run.

We operate in a world in which the perfect best reality is not discernable, and would take too long to figure out if it were. We tend to favor our desires over the limited information we get about absolute reality. When we desire something, our beliefs are shaped to get it. We believe best is what we want, and our beliefs seem reasonable to us. We act on our intuitions and desires.

Absolute reality is something we believe when we want to. It's useful when it aligns with our desires. When we can, we use it to justify our actions. Often, we twist our perception of it to fit our desires. When it contradicts our desires, we deny or discount it. People listen to their desires first, believe what they want, and use reality when they can.

Belief is personality. Belief expresses our thoughts, feelings, and desires. It is also our spiritual side. Faith is the part of our personality that interacts with our Higher Power. It responds to our body and the physical cues of our instincts. It is the software that operates our body as we do the work motivated by our beliefs.

Hunger is how the body cues the brain to the instinctive need for food. The brain begins to figure out ways to satisfy the need, and determines what it believes should be done. That belief motivates the actions that follow, which can be explained by understanding the belief.

Their hypersensitive brains and compulsion reaction create a sort of instinct peculiar to alcoholics. It functions in every way like, but is not a true, instinct. The extraordinary, intense pleasure an alcoholic's brain experiences when exposed to alcohol generates the imperative, "I Must Drink Alcohol." This compulsion functions like an instinct, as an imperative belief that drives behavior. Part of thriving for alcoholics is giving their brains the pleasure they crave. Alcoholics act on this imperative belief and respond to its physical cue, the alcohol craving, as if it were a true instinct.

Part Three: Alcoholism and Reality

301 In Defiance of Absolute Reality

Alcoholics defy reality by drinking alcohol, and this makes their lives impossible to manage. The absolute reality of life as an alcoholic is that the only solution to alcoholism is to abstain from drinking; this is the only truthful course available. The brain with which an alcoholic is born says to drink more and more alcohol, but all of life's realities must be defied to continue doing so. From the moment alcoholism is activated, compulsive use of alcohol is a problem only total abstinence can resolve. The central fact of absolute reality is that only total abstinence can solve alcoholism.

This path is not one they *believe* they ought to take, so they continue to obey the alcoholic imperative. They *believe* they must drink alcohol. The whole structure of alcoholic belief is founded on an imperative belief in the need to drink alcohol. This belief makes sense only to the alcoholic, whom non-alcoholics cannot understand because they see only the alcoholic's defiance of reality.

The mental obsession is a great helper in forming alcoholic beliefs. An opportunist, the mental obsession responds to each new situation in which alcoholics find themselves. They need beliefs to satisfy instinctual needs in each new situation. This includes normal instincts as well as the alcoholic imperative.

Normal instincts can conflict with the alcoholic imperative, but the mental obsession is always ready with handy suggestions. For example, when the normal instincts of the alcoholic signal a need for shelter and companionship, the mental obsession suggests sharing alcohol with a fellow alcoholic who has shelter. In ways like this, the mental obsession channels conflicts to satisfy the alcoholic imperative. This is how alcoholic belief gets mixed into many otherwise normal parts of alcoholics' lives. Many of the beliefs alcoholics form to satisfy normal instincts incorporate opportunities to drink alcohol. This becomes an ever greater fact in their daily life as alcoholism progresses. Alcoholics are influenced by a powerful obsession that infects every part of their lives.

There is no wrong time for an alcoholic to get sober. Every alcoholic belief is formed to excuse and enable the continued drinking that ruins an alcoholic's life. The absolute reality that only sobriety can arrest alcoholism is fact, and fact is truth. Alcoholic beliefs all defy this truth. Alcoholics sometimes have a sense of this, but remain in the grip of their alcoholism. They believe their own excuses. They believe they are managing their lives, but living in defiance of absolute reality is unmanageable. They believe they are managing their drinking, but it is running their life.

A topic often neglected in the drinking histories shared by recovering alcoholics is the monotony of alcoholism. The amount of time spent engaging in the repetitive routine of drinking is remarkable, but few alcoholics recall this monotony. The time spent drinking is one powerful way personality is shaped by alcoholism. The alcoholic is an addicted drinker of alcohol, and often not much else.

302 Alcoholism Warps Human Personality

Most alcoholics live in an alcoholic alternative reality. Their alcoholism-warped personalities create an alcoholic social reality around them. Loved ones either become enablers or are avoided. Time they could have spent being a son or daughter to a loving parent is spent drinking alone or in the company of other alcoholics. Once healthy relationships become sickened by the disease; All of the alcoholic's social relationships are affected.

Alcoholism puts loved ones in a difficult position. The most unnatural thing a person who loves another can do is to sever the relationship. The alternative is to begin enabling the alcoholism and assist in the loved one's destruction. Loved ones can practice detachment, but this is difficult even on the best days.

Alcoholics defy social reality. The nature of love makes it impossible to love, in a healthy way, persons intentionally killing themselves. People often become spiritually sick when put in that position. The social realities of loving an alcoholic are difficult to manage by non-alcoholics.

Many non-alcoholics sickened by the effects of alcoholism in a loved one begin themselves leading lives that are unmanageable. Some of them find recovery from this condition in 12 Step groups for family members. There they may also find the strength to detach with love and relate in a loving way to the alcoholic while not assisting alcoholisms destruction.

The disease presses every aspect of the alcoholics' psyche into its service. The minds of alcoholics, instead of solving the obvious problem, alcoholism, are put to work figuring out how to keep drinking. Their emotions are twisted. Loving relationships are complicated when alcoholics do not stop drinking the substance that is destroying them. The disease turns the alcoholic's own will against them. They desire to drink alcohol and are determined to continue drinking despite the trouble it causes them. Their personality shrinks as the disease progresses until they are alcoholics and not much else.

The active alcoholic is not their true self; an alcoholic's personality while in the grip of the disease is a product of the alcoholism. Alcoholism warps human personality. Alcoholics who get sober find their true selves. In sobriety they become the people they truly are.

303 The Mental Aspect of Alcoholism

Many alcoholics drink alcohol for long periods of time. The mental obsession operates freely in this environment. Allergic sensitivity increases over time with greater exposure, and alcoholism spirals out of control. Any excuse or explanation that enables continued drinking is acceptable because the brain is drugged and operating mostly on compulsion.

When reality steps in, the mental obsession is always there with an excuse. The brain, when actively drugged, wants to continue drinking, so the mind embraces these excuses. Over time, the mind turns these excuses into alcoholic beliefs.

Many of the deeply ingrained "reasons" alcoholics have for drinking began as excuses suggested by their mental obsession. The alcoholic relies on and uses them. Excuses are a type of story. With use, they become part of the alcoholic's story for why they behave as they do.

These excuses get built into the alcoholic's life narrative.

When trying to make sense of bad behavior, alcoholics use the excuses on themselves. The excuses make sense and become the alcoholic's belief about why they drink. The imperative belief that they must drink alcohol attracts these explanations and makes them part of the alcoholic belief structure.

Rational thinking is put to use calculating ways to continue drinking. The part of the personality that solves problems does not see alcoholism as a problem because the brain is drugged. Instead of solving the alcoholic's problem, the rational mind is pressed into service by the mental obsession finding ways to feed the brain the pleasure it craves.

When alcoholics are sober, the mental obsession manipulates their personality into drinking alcohol again. It tricks the rational mind into believing the problem is sobriety, and gets the mind to believe that *this time* it's okay to drink.

Actively drinking alcoholics have a faulty belief structure. The active alcoholic's belief structure enables continued drinking despite the presence of clearly known, true, and factual consequences.

The brain of the alcoholic is programmed to desire alcohol, and tends to believe the excuses provided by the mental obsession, which creates in their personality the alcoholic belief structure. Belief structures of various kinds operate in all personalities. Personality is the sum of a person's belief structures, and the active alcoholic belief structure is a fully integrated part of the alcoholic's personality.

304 Alcoholic Alternative Reality

To be believed a thing need not be true. If it serves a purpose, the mind tends to make an untruth acceptable. This tendency is greater when the untruth can serve to supply the brain with something that it compulsively desires. The rational mind may know a thing is false, but accept an excuse because the belief serves a purpose. There is a lot of this type of belief in the personality of alcoholics.

Alcoholics operating with this belief structure soon inhabit an alternative reality. They live with enablers and drink with other alcoholics. Most of their time is spent with like-minded alcoholics or alone. The social reality around them tends to support, or at least not challenge, their alcoholic worldview.

In their humanity and understanding, alcoholics know they must stop drinking, but that is not sufficient to break the mental obsession trap. They are in some ways strangers to themselves.

Many psychologists call living in an alternative reality maladjustment. Life comes with trouble even to people well adjusted to reality. The alcoholics' maladjustment becomes the source of the type of trouble only they experience. Alcoholics don't stop drinking because of this type of trouble. The alcoholic considers alcoholism related trouble unfair, and this increases their dependence on the beliefs of the alcoholic alternative reality.

The mental obsession turns this sense of unfairness, the stress of the trouble, and the trouble itself into reasons to drink alcohol. Excuses are formed around these reasons for drinking. A non-alcoholic sees the trouble as a good reason to stop, but the alcoholic sees in the trouble several good reasons to drink. The mental obsession influences alcoholics in every life situation by suggesting reasons, and twisting every bad aspect of the disease into excuses, to drink alcohol.

Resentment of the perceived unfairness fuels a motivation to drink alcohol with greater intensity. Trouble will be part of how alcoholics who get well find recovery, but for alcoholics who are drinking, trouble tends to increase drinking. Trouble deepens psychological dependence on alcohol. Troubling experiences drive the alcoholic further into alternative reality. Prolonged drinking intensifies and strengthens the mental obsession. The disease progresses as the alcoholic descends further and further into the alternative reality of active alcoholism.

This cycle of drinking strengthening the mental obsession that results in more drinking is progression. The alcoholic's day-to-day life is a living hell, downward spiraling to some inevitable bad ending.

Step One

We admitted we were powerless over alcohol- that our lives had become unmanageable.

Part Four: When Alcoholics Get Sober

401 Subconscious Beliefs Sabotage Recovery

Most alcoholics have tried many times to recover. Many were initially forced into treatment. They admitted they had a problem, but failed to get well. After that, they tried to stop drinking alcohol on their own, because they wanted to. They failed at this many times. In desperation, sincerely wanting to recover, they tried treatment again, and that, too, ended in failure. All this time a subconscious belief was forming and grew very strong; they came to believe sobriety was not possible for them.

Seeing others recover should have given them reason to believe that they, too, could recover. In fact, it strengthened their belief in their inability to recover. Their thinking was, "They can recover because they are good people. I'm a scumbag. It won't work for me." Years of experience acting on this subconscious belief over time have deeply rooted this belief in their personality. It is part of who they are and what they expect from themselves.

These alcoholics do not recover because they do not expect to recover. They base this expectation and belief on their experiences with recovery throughout their lives. It hasn't worked for them in the past, and they expect it will not this time, either. These past failures form a subconscious negative belief that sabotages every positive effort to recover. They are sincere in trying to recover, but powerful forces deep in their personality frustrate their efforts.

402 Resentment the First Experience with AA

Most alcoholics are first exposed to Alcoholics Anonymous while still drinking. The mental obsession gets an opportunity to discredit Alcoholics Anonymous before most alcoholics ever form an opinion free of its influence. Alcoholics must often overcome tricky resentments towards the fellowship and the 12 step program of recovery at the start of their involvement with Alcoholics Anonymous.

Overwhelming desperation can sometimes accomplish this by driving alcoholics to lose faith in alcohol and the excuses of the mental obsession. Those truly disgusted with their alcoholism are often the only alcoholics willing to apply honest effort to using the Alcoholics Anonymous program to recover. A little faith in Alcoholics Anonymous as a solution to their alcoholism is what keeps the newcomer sober at first. Physical age and the amount of trouble alcoholism has caused are irrelevant factors; diminishing faith in the excuses of the mental obsession and faith in Alcoholics Anonymous are the best start for recovery in AA.

403 Finding

How, then, does an alcoholic get well? Alcoholics are powerless over alcohol because their brains are hypersensitive to alcohol. Nothing can be done about that. The beliefs that enable their alcoholism are rooted in an imperative belief that acts like a true human instinct. Something *can* be done about that.

The alcoholic imperative belief can be displaced by the sober imperative belief. The alcoholic belief structure is founded on the imperative belief, "I Must Drink Alcohol." Unlike our true instincts, the alcoholic imperative belief is a faith destructive. It constantly drives the alcoholic into behaviors that contradict the human will to live.

The alcoholic imperative belief "I Must Drink Alcohol" defies absolute reality and threatens the alcoholic's existence. Active alcoholism is a constant struggle of the self destructive forces of alcoholism against the human will to live. The will to live is strong. Sobriety can displace the alcoholic imperative belief with the imperative belief, "I Must Stay Sober." This sounds theoretical, but is an accurate description of every successful recovery. Sobriety displaces alcoholism.

The process of displacement is in part a loss of faith in the motivating beliefs that drive alcohol use. The alcoholic belief structure collapses, and the will to live enables the alcoholic to begin a life in recovery. The alcoholic hits bottom and starts practicing the Alcoholics Anonymous program.

404 Before Bottom

As the disease progresses, alcoholics begin to lose faith in the destructive and irrational alcoholic belief structure. At this point, their habits are deeply ingrained and part of their life routine. No longer believing their own excuses, alcoholics continue to drink because of habit and the grip of alcoholism. In the advanced stages of the disease, alcoholics are often disgusted with what their lives have become.

Displacement often begins with a crisis of faith, called bottom. Our beliefs always seem reasonable to us until they don't. For sober beliefs to displace the belief structure of alcoholism in their personality, alcoholics must experience a loss of faith. The belief structure of active alcoholism must collapse. After that happens, if the opportunity of sober truth is available, they can find faith in sober beliefs.

Collapse need not be dramatic and alcoholics may hide it not only from others but from their own conscious self. Most alcoholics seeking help are disgusted with their alcoholism but would rather not admit they have, for years, had faith in falsehoods.

Subconscious beliefs are very powerful and bottom often begins without the alcoholic's conscious knowledge. During the last few months or years of drinking, alcoholics begin to lose faith in the beliefs that kept them drinking. Some alcoholics enter rehab, others attempt suicide, and many try hard to stop drinking on their own. These efforts are the result of the alcoholic rejecting the influence of the mental obsession. They begin to lose faith in the beliefs that kept them drinking, and the kind of thinking that forms new beliefs begins.

On a subconscious level, alcoholics become sick and tired of drinking and the trouble it causes. Their excuses become hollow and they stop using them. They may even admit they cannot understand why they can't stop. An alcoholic who is disgusted with drinking is the best candidate for sobriety.

405 The Doing is the Deciding

Our instincts are the source of our core human beliefs. When bottom is hit, the whole alcoholic belief structure collapses and the imperative belief it's founded on is exposed as a mortal threat to the alcoholic's life. The alcoholic can now embrace life. Conscious beliefs rally around the sober imperative belief, "I Must Stay Sober." This new imperative belief begins animating the personality. The alcoholic begins going to meetings and doing other things to stay sober. The sober imperative belief becomes a strong motivating force in the alcoholic's personality and thoughts of drinking are rejected.

Sober alcoholics remain powerless over alcohol, but are free of the physical craving because no alcohol is present in their body.

The construction of a sober belief structure begins with a special type of decision. An executive decision is the beginning of the actions that fulfill it. An executive decision is a belief in action: the doing is the deciding. Actions that cannot be reversed are taken, and this type of sober behavior creates faith in the decision to stay sober. Unlike alcoholics playing the rehab game, there is no Plan B. They believe in what they are doing and have faith they will be successful. Faith in their Higher Power strengthens their resolve.

This decision is a conscious act of sober belief created by the imperative belief, "I Must Stay Sober." A person who made excuses for not going to Alcoholics Anonymous now attends meetings believing they are essential to sobriety. Acting on the sober imperative belief "I Must Stay Sober" is what forms and grows the sober belief structure.

The thinking part was done when the alcoholic belief structure collapsed. The alcoholic acts on sobriety information provided by Alcoholics Anonymous. Alcoholics actively stay sober by participating in Alcoholics Anonymous groups and completing the 12 Steps with their sponsors.

Conscious beliefs are formed as actions are taken. The alcoholic created excuses after getting in trouble, and sober alcoholic beliefs form by taking action. Sober alcoholics enjoy meetings and feel better after attending them. Conscious sober beliefs are formed by this and other experiences. The experiences of life in sobriety build and shape the sober belief structure and the personality of the sober alcoholic.

Conscious beliefs become the source of sober habits. Sober alcoholics live, work, and play where they can maintain sobriety. Life choices are motivated by beliefs that originate in the imperative belief, "I Must Stay Sober."

Subconscious beliefs form as the alcoholic stays sober. Days, months, and years of sobriety form the subconscious faith in their ability to stay sober. They develop an intuition for living in harmony with others and practicing the principles of Alcoholics Anonymous.

Participating in Alcoholics Anonymous recovery is what displaces the collapsed alcoholic belief structure. Learning about recovery by studying the Big Book, attending meetings, and completing the 12 Steps with their sponsors creates sober beliefs. The new sober belief structure that occupies the controlling place in their personality is the animating force in the sober alcoholics' life.

The self-destructive beliefs of an active alcoholic are the spiritual malady of alcoholism. With the care and direction of a Higher Power, alcoholics develop a belief structure consistent with reality and spiritual health. The sober belief structure is built and maintained by completing the 12 Steps and participating in one's own recovery.

406 What Alcoholics Lose

Alcoholism warps the personality and alcoholics lose their true self. The person alcoholism creates is a shadow of the true self and has done many things that are a source of shame. Alcoholism is painful and alcoholics are uncomfortable with who they have become. It seems unfair because it is unfair; their disease made them who they are, but they endure the burden of being that person.

Unable to be their true selves, they are soon out of place. The vague feeling many alcoholics describe of never feeling comfortable is the result of this being out of place. The further down the road of alcoholism they go, the worse it gets. Alcoholics often lose first their place in their family, pulled by alcohol out of their most natural context. After that, they struggle for the illusion of normalcy. They work hard to prove to others and themselves that they are okay and can manage their drinking. During the last stages, they inhabit the most sordid of places on earth. Even those not financially ruined find they cannot buy their way out of a living hell.

Alcoholics lose many things: home, spouse, career. These things are terrible losses, but the greatest tragedy is that alcoholics lose their true self and their place in life. Alcoholics may get back a home, career, or spouse, but will find happiness only if they get back their true self and find their place in this life. This is what is meant when it's said that recovery is an inside job.

The purpose of the Alcoholics Anonymous program is to help alcoholics recover their true selves and find their place in life. Progressing through the 12 Steps is a process of shedding the personality that alcoholism twisted into its service. In sobriety, alcoholics become their true selves. With their Higher Power's guidance, they find their place in life and become who and what they truly are.

501 Faith in a Higher Power

The will of God is mysterious and requires careful discernment between the aspects that are knowable and those that are completely mysterious. It's tempting to shout that IT'S ALL MYSTERIOUS and use that to get out of trying to practice well the 11th Step. When it comes to the will of God, there are things of which we can be certain and mysteries that must be respected.

We can receive plenty of important guidance in our daily lives without ever knowing all of the will of God. Intelligent use of practical discernment leads us to the parts of the will of God that guide us and respect for the mystery of God enables us to avoid foolish self-serving guesses. When we are willing and make an honest effort, the results we get often exceed our expectations of the enlightenment we hoped to receive.

Using practical discernment we learn what the relative certainties are and act on these. I am certain that it is not the will of God that I hurt other people. Like everyone else, I learned this the hard way. If, for example, I harbor resentment against someone, I can safely assume that it is not the will of God that I harm the person I resent. Seeing that it is not the will of God to harm these people I can assume that I ought not resent them either.

As sober alcoholics, we know that we cannot drink alcohol or drugs that have a similar effect. So we are certain that self-destruction by alcoholism is not the will of God. Practical discernment reveals to us that our continued sobriety is the will of God for us. We ask for the power to carry that out.

There is a natural opposite of hurting others that reveals the deepest knowledge of the will of God. The negative power to hurt ourselves and others is matched by a positive power to live meaningful lives. The point of recovery is to find again the person we were before alcoholism took control of our lives. Building on that we find our true selves and our place in life.

I was a very selfish child. Despite that, I had strong positive qualities that alcoholism suppressed and distorted. In sobriety, these are restored and my selfishness is confronted as the root of my spiritual difficulties. For me, sobriety as a way of life is a struggle against pathological selfishness. Narcissism and grandiosity are displaced by healthy self-esteem and an honest sense of self.

Finding one's true self in sobriety is the opposite of hurting others. In sobriety we find our place in life. We become positive contributors integrated into a meaningful way of life in society.

Following the will of our Higher Power is the path to freedom. We are sober and can freely choose from the various good alternatives before us. We ask for guidance, but must decide for ourselves which path to take.

To discern these and other things requires thought, prayer, and meditation. I practice thought, prayer, and meditation often to maintain and act on the understanding arrived at through discernment.

Thought often functions as prayer and meditation in those whose beliefs don't include religious practice. Thought works with prayer and meditation in those whose beliefs do. Without trying to do God's will, we think things through and decide our best course. Doing this, we may get the same guidance we would have gotten through earnest prayer. Conscious practice is often just improving the skills we already possess.

Praying earnestly for knowledge of God's will often takes the form of carefully thinking through a situation with honest effort. Believers appeal to God. Sincere persons practicing Alcoholics Anonymous as best they can search their hearts for guidance to be true to their sober selves.

Sincere willingness and honesty keep us in accord with God's will. Maintaining the right attitude and principles makes whatever we are doing harmonious with our Higher Power.

This concept extends to the things we do to improve our conscious contact with God. Divine Truth is not something we experience or can express as absolute reality. Many spiritual experiences are emotional; we feel the Divine Presence. It's not something we can describe to someone else or even understand completely ourselves.

Whatever we do, trying to improve our conscious contact is likely to be successful in the moment and in our lives if we are sincerely willing and our efforts are honestly motivated.

One day we read from a Buddhist text and meditate on its meaning. Another day we attend a church service with a friend and are open to spiritual growth. If our attitude and motivation are right, both ought to improve our conscious contact. Our motivation and willingness have greater impact than the type of spiritual avenue we choose to travel on. We may travel a variety of spiritual paths to find our true self and discover for ourselves what we believe in spiritual matters.

I do not mean to denigrate the actions. Taking action of some form towards spiritual growth is the only way to get results. Do what you think is right. When we are sincerely willing and honestly motivated, we are not taking blind steps into the unknowable, and will learn from both successes and mistakes.

Life is complex and situations naturally arise in which we are conflicted. Discernment so clear in many situations seems to create doubt instead of certainty. There are situations in which we are sure that every course means harm, and the only certainty is that once the sun rises we are going to do something. In the midst of our perilous night, the most uncertain thing is what exactly the will of God could possibly be. We wish we knew. We want to do the right thing, but no good course can be found. In these situations, the will of God is probably not discernable. I accept that discernment is not always possible, and have faith that my Higher Power cares for me and understands my limitations.

Separating the certain from the mysterious is how we act in any case. With none of the analysis you just read in mind, have you not always acted on what you knew? Weren't you naturally passive in the face of mystery? Perhaps you rebelled against it and expressed frustration. Then you probably eventually moved on. What else could you do? Stay frustrated and miserable, that is what happens when we cannot accept painful realities?

In sobriety, we get good results with sincere willingness and honest effort. We discern what we can be certain is the direction of God, and concentrate our efforts there. None of our lapses are permanent, and we use the direction God provides to free ourselves from evil traps. Experiences good and bad will strengthen our sober belief structure as we learn from them. We find happiness in sobriety by following our Higher Power's direction and practicing the principles of the Alcoholics Anonymous program.

502 Faith in One's Self

Active alcoholism is often like being married to a terribly abusive spouse. There are intense physical beatings and that constant needling that bleeds one's self-worth. While drinking, we are constantly hammered with fact that alcohol is ruining our life, but we cannot stop drinking it. This destroys our self-confidence. I ask anyone who doubts the importance I have placed on faith in one's self to consider this: if faith in oneself is not important, why do alcohol and abusive spouses focus so much energy on destroying it?

Sobriety enables healthy self-esteem. We become confident in our decision to stay sober. We trust our intuition and the directions we get from our Higher Power. We learn to put our lives on a give and take basis. We earn our living without feeling like martyrs, often laboring with genuine enthusiasm. We share sobriety with newcomers and the alcoholics we sponsor. We develop a healthy sense of self, and sobriety is the best thing that ever happened to us. We enjoy all these things while also struggling with the pathological selfishness that afflicts alcoholics and addicts of every kind.

Some selfishness is good. We take care of our selves, pay our bills, and provide for our own needs. This requires a degree of selfishness that is healthy. If we did not take care of ourselves, we would become a burden to others and not be in a position to contribute to life in an unselfish way.

In sobriety, we find our true selves, but this process is never easy or complete. We struggle with resentment, fear, and pathological selfishness. Some of us never overcome our tendency to compensate for weakness with grandiosity. Most spiritual growth in sobriety is getting better at not letting pathological selfishness ruin our lives.

Resentment and fear are 4th Step inventory issues. These are things on which alcoholics work while progressing through the 12 Steps with their sponsors.

Pathological selfishness is the form of selfishness in our personalities that infects our stream of consciousness with the endless chatter of complaint. It's the preoccupation with self that makes sharing our lives difficult. It's the part of us that insists on managing our world instead of trusting our Higher Power's direction. It's our tendency to overindulge normal instincts like hunger and sex. We are often our own worst enemy because of the excesses of pathological selfishness.

Selfishness both good and pathological is rooted in instinct. It serves a good purpose when it creates beliefs that satisfy the needs our instincts make us aware of, without going beyond them. Most visceral belief formation is subconscious, but it can be guided by reason. Pathological selfishness can be reined in with prayer, meditation, and gratitude. Sponsors and counselors can help us when grandiosity or anger becomes a problem.

In sobriety, we find our true selves and become the people we want to be. Often, we get there by using the program to stop ourselves from being the person we ought not to be.

503 Faith in Alcoholics Anonymous

In Alcoholics Anonymous we find the solution to our alcoholism. We become part of a fellowship and find direction for our life. Alcoholics must learn to live with the absolute reality that complete sobriety must be maintained if we are to live well. The Alcoholics Anonymous fellowship is an important part of a social reality that supports that life goal.

We live in a moral universe. The physical universe is governed by laws. Some, like the law of gravity, are simple and obvious, others so complex we can only theorize as we attempt to explain them. The moral universe is like that, too. Some aspects of the good and evil in our world are easy to grasp, others impossible to understand and explain.

We develop a reasonable moral philosophy by first understanding and explaining the obvious and simple. From there, we shape an understanding of greater complexity, and respect the mystery of those things that are beyond reasonable explanation.

The core moral principle of Alcoholics Anonymous is physical sobriety. Perhaps the most simple, it is an accurate interpretation of absolute reality. The alcoholic is powerless over alcohol. The only moral course for a person in the grip of alcoholism is complete abstinence. This moral course begins with getting sober and extends into maintaining lasting sobriety. Alcoholism is the evil, sobriety the moral good. Faith in the core moral principle of Alcoholics Anonymous is the beating heart of recovery from alcoholism.

In alcoholism, we are morally lost. We more than lose our bearings; we become trapped. In every one of us there is a moral sense for good. Conscience is part of it, but there is much more to our moral sense than feeling bad when we have done wrong. We inhabit a moral universe. We interact with that aspect of our environment with our moral sense for good.

The evil of alcoholism is that it traps us in moral error. We become products of our alcoholism. Subjected to powerlessness and influenced by the mental obsession, we do many things contrary to our moral sense for good. Our desire to do otherwise is obvious. We keep trying to get back to being the person we want to be, but alcoholism keeps us trapped in moral error. Every bad thing we do is driven by the obsession and the alcoholic belief structure it creates in our personalities.

Soon after we get sober, the 12 Steps of the Alcoholics Anonymous program begin to help us recover our moral sense for good. We admit we are powerless and come to believe we can be restored to sanity. We put our lives in the care our Higher Power and begin the process of recovering our moral sense for good. We inventory our moral wrongs and correct them as best we can. We see the flaws in our character and begin the lifelong process of working on improving our character. We find our spiritual side and help others find a solution to their alcoholism. Most of early sobriety is recovering our moral sense for good. We break free of the evil that trapped us and take the 12 Steps that will enable us to lead good lives.

At some point after all that, we become mature and secure in our sobriety. We are not saints, but have recovered our moral sense for good. We lead the kinds of decent lives we desired while alcoholism had us trapped. We have a moral compass and use it to stay on our life's course.

504 The Moral Compass

The moral compass is within us, but its arrow points outside of us. It points to our worthy goals and provides the general direction towards which we ought to proceed. Being limited and imperfect, our following of its direction is like a boat or plane being piloted on a heading. Even while on course, we are subject to minor deviations, and this state is exactly what is needed to reach our worthy goals. We stay on course by means of the moment-by-moment adjustments that keep us headed in the intended direction.

The ever present requirement to endlessly make minor corrections even when on a good course informs us that absolute morality is an unreasonable expectation. We ought not to punish ourselves if we suffer from some bad decisions and moral lapses, as some degree of error is to be expected. Punishment will just waste time and energy that could be used to correct our errors and get back on course.

Human beings are inclined to seek truth and good. When misled by shortsighted, selfish beliefs, we go off the course of our moral compass towards unworthy goals. To get back on course we must use the direction of our moral compass and our Higher Powers guidance.

505 The Moral Principles We Must Live By

The direction our moral compass points to is fairly clear. Our moral compass forever points in the direction of us becoming more and more the person we have chosen to be over the course of taking the 12 Steps. Having taken the 12 Steps our personalities have been changed and we are closer to being the person we want to be. During our 4th Step we used the moral principles that are important to us to judge where and how we have been wrong. We discover for ourselves the moral principles we must live by while writing our 4th Step inventory.

These moral principles become cemented into our personality during the 5th Step. Admitting the exact nature of our wrongs in the presence of our true self, another person and God strengthens and clarifies our moral sense for good. The moral principles we must live by become a greater part of who we are by admitting the true nature of our wrongs to ourselves, another person and God. The presence of another person cements our moral principles into our social reality. Admitting the true nature of our wrongs to God has many spiritual benefits and will help us follow the guidance of our Higher Power for the rest of our lives.

Moral lapses that take us off course now are deviations from the moral principles we ourselves have chosen. Getting off our moral course is moving away from the person we really are and back to craven pathological selfishness. If we refuse to correct the course of our life we are moving back towards alcoholism. It's not assured but moral compromises tend to lead to ever greater moral compromises unless we get back on the course of our moral compass.

On track we are moment by moment becoming more and more the person we choose to be. We are guided by our moral principles and our Higher Power.

Other sensible aspects of our moral compass' direction include. Care for our human bodies; our moral compass directs us towards physical health and well being. Sobriety is another worthy goal towards which our moral compass points. Following our Higher Powers guidance by using our moral compass we avoid relapse by practicing the principles of the 12 Steps and participating in the Alcoholics Anonymous fellowship.

People's general sense of right and wrong is based on harm to others being wrong. Following our moral compass' direction guides us away from activities that harm others. Our following a positive direction is what keeps us from harming others. We avoid wrong by occupying our time doing right.

There are often several good paths available for a sober alcoholic. As we make important life choices like housing and career decisions we use our moral compass and the direction of our Higher Power. We now have powerful help when making big decisions. Having our moral compass enables each of us to establish proper directions and goals using our Higher Powers guidance.

506 Maintenance of Our Spiritual Condition

Our spiritual health is dependent on what we do. Every action we take in relation to our moral compass causes an effect in our spiritual condition.

The direction from our moral compass becomes clearer as we follow its guidance more and more closely. Positive beliefs motivating positive actions increase the ease of forming ever more positive beliefs and taking more positive actions.

The reverse of this is true when we go off course. The further off course one goes, the more unhelpful things one does and the longer one stays off course the more clouded the guidance of the moral compass becomes.

A sober alcoholic can get lost and have no clear bearing at all. One in this situation is not without direction. Abandoning the principles we learned by taking the 12 Steps leads to pain. Spiritual confusion, guilt and the effects of poorly made decisions reward those who go far off course. Absolute reality is using the pain a sober alcoholic in this situation experiences to tell them to stop doing what they know is wrong. Taking action based on the guidance of absolute reality gets us back on track. A good Alcoholics Anonymous sponsor can be very helpful in these situations.

In practice few sober alcoholics follow their moral compass to sainthood. Most sober alcoholics working a good program of action avoid getting far off course by avoiding the pain they know they will experience. Most of morality is not stepping into painful traps we know enough to stay out of. All that is required for good sobriety is avoiding the moral lapses you know will bring you pain or lead to relapse. Stay on the course your moral compass provides and enjoyment of your worthy goals will be your everyday experience.

Alcoholics who follow their moral compass enjoy happiness and peace of mind. They are better at dealing with adversity and tragedy. They sort out their difficulties with a clear unconfused mind. Their emotions experience only the true effects of their grief and their course in the wake of the tragedy is decided with their Higher Powers guidance. Alcoholics that closely follow the direction of their moral compass are steadfast companions to others in times of grief and testing.

Sober alcoholics following the direction of their moral compass and the guidance of their Higher Power are more help to others in a general way. Following ones moral compass closely is how we free ourselves from pathological selfishness. We are better able to help others when our minds are free of pathological selfishness. Even a person doing many things is less mentally busy than a person in the grip of pathological selfishness. A sober alcoholic whose mind is free of pathological selfishness is able to think about others and be present in the moment to help them. Helping others comes naturally to sober alcoholics who are guided by their Higher Power and live by moral principles.

507 Things Hinder Use of Moral Compass

The lives of many newly recovered alcoholics are such a moral shambles that they cannot see their moral compass. Time, the help of a sponsor, and active participation in Alcoholics Anonymous can help them get back on their feet and follow the direction of their moral compass.

Bad childhood religious experiences and other sources of great shame can hinder the use of ones moral compass. A tendency to constantly feel guilty introduces a dysfunctional element to the environment that causes malfunction in the system. People who continue to experience unreasonable guilt find forgiving moral direction difficult to understand and accept.

Many alcoholics are troubled by the concept of God and the authoritarian morality they were taught in childhood. Finding one's own moral compass is an alternative to an authoritarian approach to morality. Finding a loving Higher Power on one's own spiritual path is an alternative to the punishing, threatening God that frightened one as a child and in which one does not believe as an adult.

508 Sufficiently True to One's Self

We enjoy recovery from alcoholism. The continued enjoyment of sobriety requires conforming to universal morality enough to be true to ourselves. We are not saints and no one is blameless, but sincere conformity to good is a requirement for freedom from evil. We all have shortcomings and defects of character. We would not be human if we did not, but there is a moral dimension to recovery from alcoholism.

We are unable to live perfect lives, and also unable to dismiss the presence of universal morality. Our human minds may never fully understand this. God and morality are not things the human mind is able to understand completely. We acknowledge this and respect the mysteries we cannot fully understand.

Moral perfection is not possible. The sensible requirement seems to be sincerity and a willingness to follow direction. We take action by participating in the program of Alcoholics Anonymous. Plenty of imperfect people have found freedom from alcoholism in sobriety doing only that.

It has been said "we are not very good at being very bad." Some people find it difficult to accept that they are okay. Others can justify anything, but cannot escape the reality of their wrong. They trick only themselves with such moral gymnastics.

To err is human and so is the ability to think it is okay. We all seem capable of some self-justification, and maybe that serves a purpose when not taken too far.

One can be an atheist and follow one's moral compass as well as a believer. An atheist can accept this code because it is self-evident and applies without asking or needing consent. If you offend your own moral sense, destroy your body, or defy the pleading of your conscience, trouble will come to you. The directions of the moral compass lead to truth and good; ignoring them leads to lies, confusion, and trouble. Whether their confused minds know it or not, those who ignore their moral compass will be trapped by various evils.

Every alcoholic must find their way with their own moral compass. Some of us would be crushed by moral lapses others live with. In terms of morality, one must be true to one's self.

509 Complete Understanding Not Possible

Throughout this book there are themes which because of their depth defy human understanding in any complete sense. There are also limitations of language which hinder accurate descriptions of things. The reader is encouraged to find clarity about these things for themselves in thought, prayer and meditation.

We were willing and sincerely tried sobriety; now we are free of alcoholism's grip. What once seemed impossible is now ours to enjoy. Be willing and sincerely try to understand the role of faith in recovery from alcoholism. The depth of understanding you find may surprise you.

In recovery from alcoholism we experience the end of an evil. We now live in the goodness of the solution we have found. We seek to better understand the solution we have found, and be grateful for it.

510 Faith in Sober Alcoholics

Our beliefs tend to be similar to those of the people we spend time with. This is one of many reasons meetings, sponsorship, and fellowship are vital to recovery. People who stop participating in the fellowship of Alcoholics Anonymous may feel they are okay because they are keeping company with people who do not drink. The danger is that after spending a lot of time around people who do not have our problem, we come to believe we do not have our problem. Without noticing it, beliefs that got us sober no longer motivate us and the belief we can drink alcohol or use a little marijuana displace them. Sober beliefs are formed as we participate in the fellowship; they fade when we withdraw.

When I first got sober and began attending meetings, I noticed that in fellowship we all wanted something *for* one another. This spiritually healthy attitude was attractive to me.

At the end, I was living in a drug house in which everyone one wanted something *from* me and I wanted something *from* everyone else. Here was a community of people bound to one another by pathological selfishness. Negativity, mistrust, and threats were tools of survival. We all used alcohol and drugs to feel good, but felt bad most of the time.

In meetings I found the exact opposite of this situation. Everyone in meetings wanted success in sobriety for me and I wanted the same for them. We all trusted one another by sharing stories over which we would otherwise feel great shame. This was done with understanding and good-natured laughter. It was all so positive that I had to believe sobriety was possible. The spiritual sickness I lived in disappeared and was replaced by my love for the fellowship. Once in while I am asked, "Why do you still go to those meetings?" I answer, "Why wouldn't I; that's where my friends are."

601 Pathological Selfishness

Pathological selfishness, like alcohol itself, promises freedom and delivers enslavement. In our past lives as active alcoholics, it in ways acted as our Higher Power. In sobriety, it is the insidious foe embedded in our personality.

Pathological selfishness acts like a Higher Power, but is not one. Pathological selfishness leads us, but its power evaporates the second we choose not to obey it. A real Higher Power does not depend on us giving it power.

The program and fellowship of Alcoholics Anonymous always has the power, with direction and care, to lead alcoholics to sobriety. God has that power and much more. Neither ceases to be powerful as a result of anything we do. Even when under the influence, an alcoholic can transcend self and do something loving or generous. We are, even when actively drinking, able to turn off pathological selfishness. It likes to play God, but is not God. It is powerful only when we follow its lead.

Pathological selfishness likes *us* to play God, and influences us in that direction. This is the *self as general manager of the universe* aspect of what the Big Book calls self—the director forever arranging things, playing God in one's own life and with the lives of others.

We take direction from our real Higher Power. We see that playing God does not work, and stop trying to run the show. Our true selves live by the guidance we find in Alcoholics Anonymous as we practice its principles in all of our affairs. Pathological selfishness evaporates when our personalities are motivated by sober beliefs.

All of pathological selfishness is rooted in the overindulgence and distortion of our natural instincts. Even the God playing part is a distortion of our freedom to choose among various good paths. Pathological selfishness distorts this by leading us to make choices based on excessive self-interest without any guidance from moral principles. Our natural instinct to direct others when it will be helpful is distorted when we manipulate others to serve our own pathologically selfish purposes.

Pathological selfishness promises freedom, but leads to a type of enslavement. On one hand, it is freedom to do whatever we want without the constraint of moral principles. Believing we need only please ourselves, we become craven slaves of our desires in the moment, the circumstances in which we find ourselves, and what we can get out of the people in our present orbit. Without guiding principles, every natural instinct is distorted and overindulged. In the grip of pathological selfishness, we are its blind followers, slaves of our self-will.

We become free by finding and following the direction of our moral compass. We discover our true selves by taking the 12 Steps and discovering our moral principles through our relationship with our Higher Power. Only with the moral principles we have found for ourselves can we make free decisions based on what we have, in light of our true self, chosen. Guided by our Higher Power, we are free to choose from various good paths, and the principles that guide our personalities keep our relationships with others correct and good.

Sobriety in Alcoholics Anonymous is freedom from alcohol and freedom from the bondage of pathological selfishness.

602 Higher Power and Sobriety

Faith in a Higher Power occupies a special place in the life of a sober alcoholic. Not every faith object can function as a Higher Power. To function as a Higher Power, a faith object must care about the well being of the alcoholic and establish the principle requirement of sobriety, which is complete abstinence from alcohol and substances that have similar effects. Faith in God and faith in Alcoholics Anonymous play complementary roles in the lives of sober alcoholics.

God establishes the principle requirement of sobriety with absolute reality. Most alcoholics have tried to stop completely many times; all have gotten the message from absolute reality that the solution is to stop. Alcoholics Anonymous makes the message of absolute reality clear in words; it establishes sobriety's principle requirement in language an alcoholic can understand. We tell our story and make clear to newcomers that only complete abstinence will solve alcoholism.

God cares about alcoholics, and anyone who is willing to stop drinking can get well. A few alcoholics are able to get well by heeding absolute reality's message. God gave us a fellowship and a program to help many more.

The Alcoholics Anonymous fellowship and program reaches out to suffering alcoholics, welcomes them in, and offers them the solution we have found. We, as the fellowship, care about suffering alcoholics in visible ways. We communicate to them that our lives as alcoholics are just like theirs. We offer to help them solve their problem. We tell them plainly that the grip of alcoholism is strong. We make clear that lasting results will require a deep and effective personality change. We make the 12 Step program available to them.

603 A Logical Object for Faith

Alcoholism makes living very difficult, and many alcoholics who come to us feel alienated from God. Bewildered by the devastation of alcoholism, they feel God is the root of their troubles. From our own experience, we know very well how they feel, and understand, like no one else could, their confusion and despair. They remind us of what it was like for us when we first sought help from our Alcoholics Anonymous friends.

When we hit bottom and looked to Alcoholics Anonymous for help, our moral compass had been buried for years. The justifications, resentments, and rationalizations required to maintain alcoholism had obscured our moral sense for good. Many of us doubted God's love.

We saw people who had been just as hopelessly alcoholic as we had been enjoying freedom from alcoholism. These people, and the sobriety they were enjoying, represented a logical object of faith in which to believe. God seemed distant, but the efforts of our Alcoholics Anonymous friends to help us were a visible source of hope. Our Alcoholics Anonymous friends asked us in a loving way to abstain from alcohol and substances that have a similar effect. We saw the results they were getting; we hoped it would work for us. Only by seeing it work for others were we able to believe it would work for us.

The fellowship of Alcoholics Anonymous cared about us, and the program directed us to begin to abstain from alcohol and substances that have similar effects. This is how many alcoholics begin the journey to sobriety using Alcoholics Anonymous as their Higher Power. Looking back, many of us believe the love of God was working in our lives through the Alcoholics Anonymous friends who helped us find sobriety.

604 Finding God while Taking the 12 Steps

Sober belief in God often begins when our Alcoholics Anonymous friends ask us to try taking the 12 Steps. Saying the 3rd Step prayer with our sponsor, and beginning to feel our sick personalities getting well, is how many of us first experienced the faith in God we now enjoy. People feel the power of God in their emotional being. Our sober experience of God began in companionship with our Alcoholics Anonymous friends. We saw in the sobriety of our Alcoholics Anonymous friends the wellness we hoped to find, and came to believe God could restore us to sanity.

In the course of writing our 4th Step inventory, we begin to personally relate to God as Our Higher Power. We need moral direction as we face our faults, and conscience alone is an inadequate guide to rediscovering our moral sense for good. During this time, the concept of an authoritarian God making impossible demands for perfection may be displaced by a Loving Higher Power, a reasonable and effective God who objects to the wrongs in our past, but understands our humanity and leads us to a better way to live.

As we read our 5th Step, the forgiveness of God is felt. We are reading it to a person, but through our emotions we feel the love and caring of our Higher Power. In the hour that follows the 5th Step, we bask in the experience of Our Higher Power's love.

We began our spiritual journey with faith in our Alcoholics Anonymous friends. We now believe in God and Alcoholics Anonymous. As we work through the character building steps, the humanity of the fellowship and personality changing power of the program are the means our Loving Higher Power uses to build our sober character structure.

The foundation of the sober belief structure is faith in God. Our Higher Power inspires us to participate in Alcoholics Anonymous and practice the principles of the 12 Step program. We arrange our lives around sobriety and the guidance provided by Our Higher Power.

We ask God to remove our character defects. Practicing the principles of Alcoholics Anonymous in all of our affairs builds our sober character structure with the help of our moral sense for good, the guidance of our Higher Power, and the help of our sponsor. We now follow the direction of Our Higher Power, and this enables us to make amends. Our moral sense for good enables us to use the direction of our moral compass. We stop creating wreckage.

605 Stabilizing Effect of Faith in AA

The cornerstone of Alcoholics Anonymous spirituality is freedom of belief. We must discover personal belief for ourselves. There is no theology in Alcoholics Anonymous. This is a blank space only the individual member can fill, and the forms of faith that fill it can change over time.

Faith in Alcoholics Anonymous has a stabilizing effect on personal spirituality. We may develop faith in a religious organization and become part of a fellowship of religious believers. This can and often does become a meaningful lifelong way for a sober alcoholic to enjoy spirituality.

For sober alcoholics who outgrow that form of faith by discovering deeper personal beliefs that contradict the organization's dogma, faith in Alcoholics Anonymous can see them through this crisis. After this phase, they may not return to any religious fellowship, or they may find one in agreement with their deeper personal beliefs. Either way, Alcoholics Anonymous is there for them as an object of faith stabilizing whatever spiritual choice they make.

Other sober alcoholics explore numerous spiritual teachings to improve their conscious contact with their Higher Power. They form all sorts of beliefs using a wide variety of sources. They find inspiration everywhere. In Alcoholics Anonymous, they are free to discuss how any or all of these beliefs help them maintain sobriety. Keeping Alcoholics Anonymous and sobriety at the center of their spiritual experience stabilizes it and enables them to be inspired by the good things they see in every faith.

Some Alcoholics Anonymous members are agnostic in their personal faith, but have no objection to the word God in the 12 Steps. They do not believe any detailed theology about God is possible. They enjoy and are encouraged by spiritual feelings. They believe God is experienced mostly by our feelings, and avoid fixed ideas about the nature of God. They avoid any sort of religious argument, believing no one can know or be *right* in matters of God. They may consider themselves agnostics, pantheists, or deists, but many choose no label at all.

The God of the 12 Steps is the personal Creator God of Western thought common in our culture. This view of divinity is not universal. This way of looking at God is not shared by large parts of the world's population. Hinduism, Buddhism, Daoism, and Jainism are examples of faiths with millions of members that influence the social cultures of entire nations. There is no shortage of alcoholics within these populations.

Rather than say they are non theistic, a better understanding of these faiths comes from looking at what they do believe. For example, Jainism believes that the universe is eternal. In the belief structure of Jainism, no act created the world; it has always been. This belief has no direct impact on any of the 12 Steps, but it is part of a belief structure in which divinity differs from the personal Creator God of the Big Book. Holding the principle of freedom of belief, we must accept the fact that not all religions share belief in a personal Creator God.

Some Heroin Anonymous members practice these faiths; others find inspiration and adopt some of their practices. To accommodate this, the 12 Step program is adaptable in a variety of ways, with varying results depending on the Step. For example, Buddhism's emphasis on meditation is often considered an asset in practicing Step 11. Many Alcoholics Anonymous members who are enthusiastic about a wide variety of faiths appreciate and practice Buddhist meditation.

Freedom of belief in practice allows anyone to adapt the program to suit a particular faith. We freely allow anyone to practice our program in the manner of their own choosing.

There are, and always have been, Alcoholics Anonymous members who want to have nothing to do with God. We continue to welcome them, and their ongoing participation in the fellowship is evidence that the principle of freedom of belief is practiced, in fact, by the Alcoholics Anonymous fellowship.

In Alcoholics Anonymous, freedom of belief is a great strength. We exist to help anyone who comes to us recover from alcoholism. We believe that abstinence from alcohol and substances that have similar effects is required for an alcoholic's sobriety, but welcome those who still struggle with active alcoholism. The effectiveness of our program is based on sincere personal willingness. The near total freedom of belief ensures that no one feels forced, there are no rules to defy, and all are free in sobriety to find and be their true selves.

606 Belief is Motivation

There is no greater object for faith in Alcoholics Anonymous than genuine evidence of recovery from alcoholism. To form the sober belief that they, too, can get well, newcomers must see in us the freedom from alcoholism they crave. Driven by their will to live, the core imperative belief of sobriety can take shape and become their motivation. Seeing evidence of sobriety, they come to believe they too can get well. Driven by their will to live, they come to believe that they must stay sober.

We ought to be tactful and genuine in our efforts with newcomers. Ours is a spiritual program, and we ought not to be shy about who and what we are. We are sober today because God has given us a program of action and personality change. Participate in Alcoholics Anonymous and newcomers will see that your personality has been changed for the better.

Alcoholism often alienates newcomers from God. This antipathy is mostly between themselves and God. Most have no objection to the beliefs of others, if they are genuine and tactfully presented. Tell the story of your sobriety, and let newcomers form the belief they, too, can have a story of sobriety if they work for it.

Ours is a program of personality change. The disease of alcoholism infects every aspect of our personality. In the grip of the disease, we are programmed to drink alcohol. Physically we are powerless because we are hyper sensitive to the pleasurable effects of alcohol and taking even one single drink unleashes a physical craving for more. Our personality after years of suffering active alcoholism is in large part a product of our disease because it was shaped under the influence of the mental obsession. We cannot do anything to change our physical powerlessness but we can get sober and change our personality. We must shed the alcohol obsessed diseased personality and recover our true selves with Alcoholics Anonymous as our method and our guide.

We follow the 12 Steps and our Higher Power to effect a personality change sufficient to maintain recovery from alcoholism. If our belief structure does not change, we soon return to alcoholism no matter how great our desire to escape it might have been for a time. We must become sober alcoholics motivated by sober beliefs if we are to stay well.

Sober alcoholics lives have been changed in several important ways by taking the 12 Steps. Sober alcoholics are motivated by sobriety's core imperative belief. Sober alcoholics have recovered their moral sense for good, which enables them to see what is true and false in life as a recovering alcoholic. Sober alcoholics have and use their moral compass to steer towards their own worthy goals. Sober alcoholics have found their true selves and are the people they've chosen to be. A sober alcoholic is someone a newcomer can look to and say, "I want that!

Freedom from alcoholism and the freedom to be the person I choose to be."

607 Respecting the Mystery

In spiritual matters we know that we do not have all the answers and do not have the right to expect others to believe as we do. Discovering for ourselves who God is to us personally is part of our respecting the mystery of God. Respecting the conception of God others form and use as their Higher Power is another way we respect the mystery of God.

The most important spiritual thing one can know is that complete knowledge of God is beyond human understanding. Even our partial knowledge is colored by the beyond human understanding nature of God. This fact is the beginning of spiritual knowledge. Respect for the limitations of human understanding in discovering spiritual beliefs for ourselves is the core of respecting the mystery of God.

In this book belief and faith are used to explain human behavior around alcohol and alcoholism. There is much we still do not understand about our fellow alcoholics and ourselves. Finding our moral compass and our true selves in sobriety were steps in the right direction. There are many things about ourselves we still do not understand. Facing behaviors and circumstances we wish could be changed forces us to respect the mystery of life. We are grateful for the ability to change the things we can. We are grateful for our own sobriety.

In Alcoholics Anonymous meetings we befriend alcoholics in need of sobriety that we hope will find lasting recovery; we are disappointed when they do not. Loved ones we know well suffer tragedies despite our efforts to help them. The cold impersonal fact that a loved one may not get well forces us to respect the mystery of alcoholism and recovery from it. We ask ourselves why God made life challenging and difficult. If God, Our Creator, wanted life to be easy for us, it would be. Difficult things like alcoholism are part of life for reasons that are mysterious. We respect these mysteries and by doing this we respect the mystery of God.

Faith in Alcoholics Anonymous

The true solutions we find for our difficulties are often embedded within the difficulties themselves. Embedded in alcoholism is the clear, absolute reality that only complete abstinence can solve it. We find the means to live in harmony with this reality in Alcoholics Anonymous. In this sense, Alcoholics Anonymous comes to us from God. Alcoholics Anonymous is one way God directs and cares for alcoholics. Our faith in Alcoholics Anonymous is in this sense faith in God. We believe in God by believing in the solution Our Creator has given us. We have faith in Alcoholics Anonymous.

Afterword:

Alcoholics Anonymous members use the Big Book of Alcoholics Anonymous as a guide for how to complete the 12 Steps of recovery. This little book is the "why" to the Big Book's "how." Recovery from a disease that is part of our constitution from birth, no more our choice than the color of our eyes and deeply ingrained in the visceral beliefs that motivate our personality, requires a deep and effective reorganization of our personality.

Active sobriety must displace drinking alcohol as the defining characteristic of our identity. We must become Sober Alcoholics in the living breathing sense of those words.

The 12 Steps are how we do that. They are how we shed the warped alcohol obsessed personality that keeps us trapped in alcoholism. During the course of taking the 12 Steps we find our true selves and become the person we choose to be. The drinking alcoholic personality was in large part a product of the disease alcoholism. The sober alcoholic is in large part a product of ones program of recovery. Sober beliefs are built by participating in our own recovery. The experience of taking the 12 Steps directs and accelerates personality change. The lasting beliefs that create the sober personality form over time with experience as we participate in our own recovery.

As alcoholics, our only course to living in harmony with absolute reality is total abstinence from the use of alcohol and substances that have similar effects. Positive faith in sobriety becomes the core motivating belief of our personality. It shapes our lives around our will to live. We recover who we are and become the people we are meant to be by obeying our core imperative belief, "I Must Stay Sober."

The Pamphlets

Discovering Your Beliefs
Positive Beliefs; Positive Actions
Step Three
Pathological Selfishness – The Anti Higher Power
Allergy, Mental Obsession and Recovery from Alcoholism

Discovering Your Beliefs

Alcoholics Anonymous challenges us to discover for ourselves what we believe. We begin by understanding what we know to be true, and build on that foundation of truth.

We know alcoholics in Alcoholics Anonymous are staying sober. Alone, without support or guidance, we were never able to stop drinking alcohol. We understand that with Alcoholics Anonymous sobriety is possible, and build on that foundation of truth.

The Alcoholics Anonymous program of recovery is spiritually powerful and can be used as a Higher Power. Everyone involved in the Alcoholics Anonymous program believes in its power to help them stay sober. This is as true of Alcoholics Anonymous members who believe in God as of those who do not. We all believe the program of Alcoholics Anonymous is the path to lasting sobriety.

Alcoholics Anonymous encourages everyone to discover spirituality for themselves. It never asks that you believe anything you find unbelievable.

Sobriety can be challenging. We emerge from intoxication into a new life of sobriety, and find that we are confused. This is to be expected. We never gave clear thought to what we believe, and years spent as alcoholics have left us unprepared for life without alcohol.

Spiritual principles can appear difficult to understand and impossible to do. For example, who can know the will of God? It's easy to feel overwhelmed when something seems impossible.

What do we already know that can guide us? We know that it is wrong to harm others. It's clear from the start that God's will is that we do no harm. Sobriety is one way we do no harm to ourselves or to others. Doing what is needed to stay sober and helping others stay sober is doing the will of God.

When we are sincere in our willingness and the motivation for our efforts is honest, we are not taking blind steps into the unknowable. We know our part has been an honest one, and we will learn from both successes and mistakes. Sincere willingness and honest effort guide us.

The best way to discover your beliefs is to practice the Alcoholics Anonymous program. To stay sober, it's strongly suggested that you attend meetings, get a sponsor, and read the Big Book. Your beliefs will take shape as you do these things. As we participate in Alcoholics Anonymous, we learn what we believe and our attitudes begin to change.

With our sponsor's help, we learn about our problem and the solution. We no longer face our alcoholism alone. Together with people who have found a solution, we face it with hope and our Higher Power's help. Our belief in the Alcoholics Anonymous solution to our alcoholism grows as we take the twelve steps with our sponsor's guidance.

A garden left untended is soon a patch of weeds. Good recovery doesn't just happen. It is always the result of honest effort.

Positive Beliefs, Positive Actions

Try not doing anything. See how long you can remain inactive. Not long, because you are human and humans do things. We thrive. The basis of sobriety is a life of activity free of alcohol and substances like it. Sobriety is how alcoholics are able live today, and because of the 12 Steps it is also why they live today.

We have turned our wills and our lives over to our Higher Power. Our chosen professions, friendships, and good habits are guided by our Higher Power. Don't doubt this. Positive beliefs in your Higher Power's guidance are a great source of strength. Sobriety does not make life easy, but we often find the harder path of responsibility leads us clear of the awful consequences of drinking.

Seek out and befriend other alcoholics who are enjoying happy sobriety in Alcoholics Anonymous. Develop habits of activity and social interaction that include meetings and the other things you are doing to maintain sobriety. Discover for yourself ways to nurture positive sober beliefs. Develop and follow your interests in spiritual understanding.

People shape one another's beliefs. Be a positive force in the sobriety of others, and find strength in friendship with others who are enjoying sobriety. Sober alcoholics need fellowship. Alcoholics who spend too much time with people who do not have our problem come to believe they do not have our problem. They think they ought to be like the people they are with, and decide to have a few beers or use a little marijuana. For better or worse, people shape one another's beliefs.

Our alcoholism brought us to the brink of destruction, but our human will to live drove us to find a new life in sobriety. In Alcoholics Anonymous, we found a program of action. We did what others had done to be free of alcoholism. Our alcoholism was displaced by sobriety. The only sure way not to do a thing is to be constantly doing something else. Practicing the principles of the 12 Steps in everything we do is the activity that displaces active alcoholism.

We complete the 12 Steps with the help of our sponsor. Our lives are then on a new foundation. We choose our paths in life based on our Higher Power's direction. Our lives are based on positive beliefs that motivate positive actions.

STEP THREE

The most frightening thing about God is not what scared us about Him as children. Our biggest fear is what God might ask us to do now. We fear God will ask too much and that we won't be able to do what He asks. The Third Step appears to confirm this fear. "...turn our will and our lives over to the care of God *as we understood Him*".

This seems to go far beyond asking too much by asking for everything, everything I want, my will, everything I have, my life. Will these things no longer be mine? It's easy to see how someone might object to this idea.

We take the Third Step at the beginning of our sobriety. Giving up our will at that time is giving up our desire and determination to drink alcohol. Giving up our life at that time is giving up our life as an alcoholic. We are asked to give up a life controlled by alcoholism. We turn over to our Higher Power a life that we no longer control.

We turn our obsessive desire to drink and our life as an alcoholic over to our Higher Power. By giving our old life to our Higher Power, we begin life anew. We do this so we can begin finding a life of our own, free of alcohol. We find this life in the twelve-step program of Alcoholics Anonymous.

We could try to take the steps alone, but it is greatly suggested that we find a sponsor to help us. With our sponsor's help we clear up the mess we have made of our lives and repair our relationships with loved ones. The only thing most of our loved ones want for us is to be free of alcohol, to be the person they know and love.

With our personalities and relationships adjusted by the twelve steps, we receive intuitive direction from God. Our Higher Power guides us when we ask to know His will for us and to be granted the power to carry it out.

We know God wants us to stay sober. Everything we already do to maintain our sobriety is the will of Our Higher Power. Going to meetings, sponsorship, and helping other alcoholics get sober are all the will of our Higher Power.

Our Higher Power is not a navigation system that provides turn-by-turn instructions. As free persons we must take the initiative. Having cleared away the mess and dedicated our lives to sobriety, our motives are sincere. We make honest efforts based on these motives and take responsibility for ourselves. We learn from our mistakes and build on our successes.

We know hurting others is not the will of Our Higher Power. The opposite of hurting others is finding our place in this life; the productive role we are going to play is will of our Higher Power. The point of sobriety is that we recover who we were and become the person we ought to be. This is a different thing for each of us, and we use our Higher Power's direction to find our true selves.

Pathological Selfishness

Pathological selfishness, like alcohol itself, promises freedom and delivers enslavement. In our past lives as drinking alcoholics, it acted as our Higher Power. In sobriety, it is the insidious foe embedded in our personality.

Pathological selfishness acts like a Higher Power, but is not one. Pathological selfishness leads us, but its power evaporates the second we choose not to obey it. A real Higher Power does not depend on us giving it power.

The program and fellowship of Alcoholics Anonymous always has the power, with direction and care, to lead alcoholics to sobriety. God has that power and much more. Neither ceases to be powerful as a result of anything we do. Even when under the influence, an alcoholic can transcend self and do something loving or generous. We are, even when actively drinking, able to turn off pathological selfishness. It likes to play God, but is not God. It is powerful only when we follow its lead.

Pathological selfishness likes *us* to play God, and influences us in that direction. This is the *self as general manager of the universe* aspect of what the Big Book calls self—the director forever arranging things, playing God in one's own life and with the lives of others.

We take direction from our real Higher Power. We see that playing God does not work, and stop trying to run the show. Our true selves live by the guidance we find in Alcoholics Anonymous as we practice its principles in all of our affairs. Pathological selfishness evaporates when our personalities are motivated by sober beliefs.

All of pathological selfishness is rooted in the overindulgence and distortion of our natural instincts. Even the God playing part is a distortion of our freedom to choose among various good paths. Pathological selfishness distorts this by leading us to make choices based on excessive self-interest without any guidance from moral principles. Our natural instinct to direct others when it will be helpful is distorted when we manipulate others to serve our own pathologically selfish purposes.

Pathological selfishness promises freedom, but leads to a type of enslavement. On one hand, it is freedom to do whatever we want without the constraint of moral principles. Believing we need only please ourselves, we become craven slaves of our desires in the moment, the circumstances in which we find ourselves, and what we can get out of the people in our present orbit. Without guiding principles, every natural instinct is distorted and overindulged. In the grip of pathological selfishness, we are its blind followers, slaves of our self-will.

We become free by finding and following the direction of our moral compass. We discover our true selves by taking the 12 Steps and discovering our moral principles through our relationship with our Higher Power. Only with the moral principles we have found for ourselves can we make free decisions based on what we have, in light of our true self, chosen. Guided by our Higher Power, we are free to choose from various good paths, and the principles that guide our personalities keep our relationships with others correct and good.

Sobriety in Alcoholics Anonymous is freedom from alcohol and freedom from the bondage of pathological selfishness.

Allergy, Mental Obsession and Recovery

Faith is not always a positive force for good in our personalities. The things we choose to believe can destroy us. The mental obsession of alcoholism creates in the alcoholic a self-destructive belief structure. Its beliefs become the alcoholics' motivation and enable the excuse making that keeps the alcoholic actively drinking long past the beginning of alcoholism related problems

Alcoholics are born with a physical sensitivity to alcohol. We call it an allergy. One aspect of an allergy is sensitivity to the allergen. Some allergics are sensitive when very young and it's easy to say they are born with it because there was never a time when they were not sensitive. Others become obviously sensitive later in life. In both cases the sensitivity increases with time and exposure. Those who become sensitive later might think it began with exposure but they were probably born with the tendency to become sensitive.

The place where misunderstanding begins with calling alcoholism an allergy is the type of reaction. Those allergic to pollen or types of food experience painful symptoms and this naturally motivates them to avoid the allergic substance. With alcohol the part of the body affected is the brain and the effect is pleasurable. Other allergies create thoughts of aversion and ones' brain thinks how to avoid exposure. Alcohol creates pleasure in the brain. This reaction in the brain creates thoughts of how to get more.

Those born without sensitivity to alcohol experience pleasure but not at the same level: Exposure does not create or increase compulsion in their personalities.

The mental result of most allergies is repulsion; to clean it off and stay away from the allergen. The mental result of the alcohol allergy is compulsion; the brain says give me more and when can I do this again. This compulsion reaction creates in the personality of the alcoholic a mental obsession for more alcohol. There is in the mind of the alcoholic an obsession that generates endless reasons to and excuses for drinking alcohol.

Alcoholism is progressive in several ways. Sensitivity increases over time with exposure and alcoholism spirals out of control. The more the alcoholic drinks the more the alcoholic wants to drink. Because drinking increases sensitivity this makes the mental obsession stronger. If reality steps in the mental obsession is always there with an excuse and excuses, once accepted, double as reasons. The brain under the influence of alcohol is programmed to desire alcohol believes the excuses provided by the mental obsession. Belief motivates action.

The excuse making part of the mental obsession is what creates in the personality of the alcoholic the alcoholic belief structure. Belief structures of various kinds operate in all of our personalities. Personality is just an overall belief structure and the alcoholic belief structure is a fully integrated part of the alcoholics' personality.

One must remember that to be believed a thing need not be true. If it serves a purpose the mind tends to make a thing acceptable. The rational mind may know it is false but accept an excuse because the belief serves a purpose. There is a lot of this type of belief in the personality of alcoholics. It is the alternative reality of alcoholism. At times alcoholics may know their alcoholism lies but that is not sufficient to break the mental obsessions trap.

The alcoholic mentally speaking lives in an alternative reality. Psychologists call this maladjustment.

Life comes with trouble even when one is well adjusted to reality but the alcoholics' maladjustment becomes the source of an extra dose of trouble. The alcoholic considers this very unfair and this increases dependence on the beliefs of alcoholic alternative reality.

Alcoholics don't suddenly decide to stop drinking because an extra dose of trouble comes their way. The mental obsession turns the sense of unfairness, the stress of the trouble and the trouble itself into both reasons to drink and excuses for doing so. A non-alcoholic sees the trouble as one good reason to stop drinking but the alcoholic sees the trouble as several good reasons to drink more. Resentment of unfairness fuels a motivation to drink alcohol with greater intensity.

Trouble will be part of how those alcoholics who get well find recovery but when alcoholics are drinking trouble tends to increase their drinking and dependence on alcohol. Troubling experiences drive the alcoholic further into alternative reality and increased drinking intensifies the strengthening of the mental obsession. The alcoholics' day to day life is just a living hell; downward spiraling to some kind of bad ending.

Some alcoholics' do recover from this hopeless condition.

If you admit that you are an alcoholic and clearly see the mental obsession turning things into excuses for and reasons to drink alcohol. If you admit this has made your life unmanageable then you may want to take part in the solution we have found. We are just like you except that we have found a solution for our alcoholism and want to help you find the solution for your alcoholism.

Talk to a Alcoholics Anonymous sponsor about recovery from alcoholism. Attend Alcoholics Anonymous meetings as often as you can and do as your sponsor suggests.

The fellowship of Alcoholics Anonymous exists to help you find and enjoy recovery from alcoholism. Keeping company with and making friends of other people like you dedicated to not drinking alcohol is vital for recovery. Alcoholics adrift in the world without the support and friendship of other sober alcoholics drink again. This is one of alcoholisms obvious realities. Your chances of recovering from alcoholism alone are not good as your experience up till now likely proves

The 12 Step program of Alcoholics Anonymous can break the spell of the mental obsession. Lifesaving truth is much stronger than the lies of the mental obsession. A beginning can be made simply by believing what you see with your own eyes. We are alcoholics just like you who have broken free from the trap of alcoholism. Simply believe the solution we have found can work for you. Desire sobriety and be willing to try the solution we have found.

For now just believe in Alcoholics Anonymous. That can be your Higher Power. Alcoholics Anonymous is a Higher Power active in the life and beliefs of everyone who recovers. Those who believe in God believe in Alcoholics Anonymous also.

Step One: We admitted we were powerless over alcohol–that our lives had become unmanageable.

Step Two: Came to believe that a Power greater than ourselves could restore us to sanity.

Get an Alcoholics Anonymous sponsor, attend meetings, participate in the fellowship and take the steps with your sponsors help.

Alone we die: Together we recover.